The Scandal of Service

THE SCANDAL OF SERVICE

JESUS WASHES OUR FEET

Jean Vanier

NOVALIS

CONTINUUM - NEW YORK

Novalis
49 Front Street East , Second Floor
Toronto, Ontario, M5E 1B3
Canada

The Continuum Publishing Company
370 Lexington Avenue
New York, NY 10017
United States of America

This edition published in Canada by Novalis, Saint Paul University, Ottawa and in the USA by the Continuum Publishing Company.

Second printing 1998.

Originally published in 1996 by Novalis, Saint Paul University.

Cover: Robert Paquette
Layout: Gilles Lepine

Printed in Canada.

ISBN 2-89088-783-9 (Novalis)
ISBN 0-8264-1105-3 (Continuum)

Canadian Cataloguing in Publication Data

Vanier, Jean, 1928-
            The scandal of service: Jesus washes our feet

(L'Arche collection)
Translation of: Aimer jusqu'au bout.
ISBN 2-89088-783-9

            1. Footwashing (Rite). 2. Caring—religious aspects—Christianity. 3. Humility—Christianity. 4. Arche (Association).
5. Mentally handicapped—Services for. I.Title. II. Series.

BV873.F3V3513 1996 265'.9 C96-900588-1

Library of Congress Catalog Card Number 98-73251

*My special thanks go to the following persons
who helped me
with the contents of this book
or to improve the English:*

Fr. Nicholas Hudson

Alison Bell

Fr. Brendan Kelly

Fr. Gaetano

CONTENTS

THE WASHING OF THE FEET IN L'ARCHE

The fact that Jesus washed his disciples' feet may seem to some people a simple, ordinary gesture; to others it is something shocking and challenging. In L'Arche we consider the washing of the feet to be an important and highly significant act.

L'Arche was founded in 1964, when I invited Raphael Simi and Philippe Seux[1] to live with me. Our home was a small house that I had been able to purchase through the help of friends. These two men had been shut up in a rather violent institution after their parents died. My intention was to create community with them, to help them find a more human existence.

---

[1] See *The Story of L'Arche* and *The Spirituality of L'Arche* in the Novalis *L'Arche Collection.*

In L'Arche, people with mental handicaps live together with "assistants," people who want to share their lives with them and become their friends. We live in small houses, well integrated into a village or a city neighbourhood. People who are weak and fragile obviously need the help of those who are stronger. In L'Arche, however, we are discovering that the opposite is equally true: people who are stronger need those who are more fragile. We need one another.

People who are powerless and vulnerable attract what is most beautiful and most luminous in those who are stronger: they call them to be compassionate, to love intelligently, and not only in a sentimental way. Those who are weak help those who are more capable to discover their humanity and to leave the world of competition in order to put their energies at the service of love, justice and peace. The weak teach the strong to accept and integrate the weakness and brokenness of their own lives which they often hide behind masks.

A few years ago we welcomed Loïc into one of our homes in Trosly-Breuil (France). Today Loïc is forty years old, but he looks like a child of five. He is small, weak, cannot talk and is limited in his capacity to understand. But Loïc has a sensitive, loving heart; he senses immediately whether or not the person next to him is open, attentive and loving. I lived for a year in his house, "La Forestière," and, though we live in different houses today, we still remain close. Loïc taught me to be more attentive and loving; he opened my heart and the intelligence of my heart. Even though I can still encounter today the temptations to seek success and recognition, he brought down many of my defence mechanisms and my need always to have the last word.

People who are weak and vulnerable can also awaken in us what is most dark and ugly. Their cry, their provocations, their constant demands and their depression can unmask our own anguish and violence. But isn't it true that in order to grow in our humanity, we need to recognize the violence and the power of hatred within our own heart, all that we consider shameful and try to hide? In L'Arche, we are gradually learning how to manage these fears and energies in a positive way, and how to free ourselves from the powers of destruction within us.

One of the dangers of society today is over-emphasizing people's need for independence and autonomy through competence and strength, and playing down the more basic need of everyone for relationship. We attain human maturity as we live relationships more deeply and become open to others and ready to serve them. Are we not all responsible for the creation of a world where there is more solidarity and friendship? If we close ourselves up, we smother our hearts and the energy of love within us. We treat others indifferently. All this leads to vast inequalities between the weak and the strong, and finally to jealousy, hatred, war and death.

Community life in L'Arche is founded on heart-to-heart relationships and the joy of recognizing our common humanity. We are discovering that relationship begins with an attitude of receptivity, and by welcoming others, listening to them, and trusting them. This leads to communion, which is the to-and-fro of love, where each person gives and each one receives. Communion is a place of mutual trust and respect. It implies humility, openness, vulnerability, a sharing not only of one's gifts and wealth, but also one's poverty and limits.

In communion, we must speak, so that we may share our ideas, our faith, our hopes, our difficulties and our limits. Non-verbal communication is also important. Through the love in our eyes, the way we touch, our tone of voice, and with our whole body, we can and do express our compassion, our needs, our difficulties, and our pain. People can hide who they really are behind words, ideas, theories, their function and their authority. Their real personality comes through their gestures, their facial expressions, and the way they welcome others and create friendships.

People with handicaps are often discouraged. For years they have been regarded as disappointments, "misfits" with little or no value. In response to these negative attitudes, they tend to lose all confidence in themselves and to see themselves as ugly and useless. They can even feel guilty for existing. In order to help them, or others who are discouraged, we need to be attentive to them, to love them and to trust in their capacity to do things. To love someone does not mean first of all to do things for that person; it means helping her to discover her own beauty, uniqueness, the light hidden in her heart and the meaning of her life. Through love a new hope is communicated to that person and thus a desire to live and to grow. This communication of love may require words, but love is essentially communicated through non-verbal means: our attitudes, our eyes, our gestures and our smiles. This is the whole pedagogy of L'Arche, which we try to put into practice in spite of all our inadequacies.

L'Arche and the Gospel

Living in L'Arche with men and women who have handicaps, who are sometimes deeply wounded, fragile and suffering, has helped me to discover the message of Jesus, the Good News of love, in a completely new way. The gospel message gave me the strength to begin L'Arche, but life in L'Arche revealed to me the deep, hidden meaning of the Gospels.

Jesus speaks mainly to the poor, the rejected and the powerless. He says explicitly that he came to announce Good News to the poor (Luke 4). Those who are poor and humble feel loved and understood by Jesus. He touches and awakens their hearts, he reassures them and loves them; they in turn respond with love. People who are well-situated in society, who know success, who have a certain influence and who exercise authority, but who are not in touch with their inner weaknesses and poverty, have trouble understanding the loving but demanding message of Jesus. He disturbs them. In the parable of the wedding feast (Luke 14), the poor, the crippled, the lame and the blind respond to the invitation to come. The rich and powerful refuse. They do not have time because they have other things to do. They are often seeking the *knowledge* of God, but their hearts are not humble and open enough simply to welcome the *presence* of God.

My experience in L'Arche has shown me that many people who are limited in their capacities of understanding have humble, loving hearts that are open to Jesus' message. However, many people who are quite capable intellectually are intolerant, self-satisfied and prejudiced against others who are "different."

This is surely what Paul expresses in 1 Corinthians 1:26, drawing from his own experience in the creation of communities: God has chosen what is foolish and weak in the world, those of humble

birth, who are looked down upon, in order to con-
found the wise and the strong of this world.

Jesus affirms: "When you give a dinner or a
banquet, do not invite your friends or your brothers
or your relations or rich neighbours, lest they also
invite you in return, and you be repaid. But when
you give a feast, invite the poor, the maimed, the
lame and the blind, and you will be blessed" (Luke
14:12-14).

The vocation of L'Arche is to eat at the same
table as people with mental handicaps. We may not
all have Christian faith and we may not all go to
church, but we can all eat around the same table. By
calling us to sit at the same table, Jesus is asking us
to become friends, to create a new family with each
other.

And Jesus goes even further. He not only
becomes a friend of the poor, he identifies with
them: "Whoever welcomes one of these little ones
in my name, welcomes me" (Luke 9), and, "Whatever you do to the least of my brothers and sisters,
you do to me" (Matthew 25). In L'Arche, as we let
people like Loïc awaken and nourish our hearts, we
begin to enter into this mystery. We discover that,
little by little, they are transforming us and leading
us into the world of tenderness, inner peace and
compassion. They bring us closer to Jesus.

The Washing of the Feet: A Paraliturgy

The Gospels show us how Jesus came to change our hearts. The washing of the feet is not first and foremost an act we all have to imitate. It reveals how Jesus is calling all his disciples to an inner attitude of service and love in all things. However, in L'Arche we have discovered how important it is also actually to wash each other's feet.

If I remember correctly, our community in Liverpool (U.K.) was the first to live this liturgy in L'Arche. The community leader told me how all the members of one household had washed each other's feet and how they had lived this in a spirit of prayer and silence. She said that it had helped each one to enter more deeply into the mystery of Jesus' death and resurrection. The following year, on Maundy Thursday, we performed this same paraliturgy in the household where I was living in Trosly. Little by little, this paraliturgy has become part of the Holy Week celebrations in each of our L'Arche houses.

On Maundy Thursday in Trosly, we start with the Eucharist for the whole community. Then in each house we celebrate the paschal meal: we eat the paschal lamb in a spirit of thanksgiving. During the meal, we take time so that each person around the table can talk about his or her past and share the sorrows and joys of the previous year. We give thanks to God for his guidance over the year. Then, when the meal is over, we all go into the next room where we sit in a circle in prayerful silence.

After singing a hymn that brings us all together and leads us into an attitude of prayer, the house leader reads the text of John (13:1-17). Then the house leader kneels down in front of the person on the right and washes his or her feet gently, tenderly. Once the first person's feet have been washed, the one who has received this service places his or her hands on the head of the person who has washed the feet. They pray silently; this signifies the gratitude and desire to live in communion with the one whose feet have been washed. Following this, the house leader sits down and the one who has just had his or her feet washed kneels down and washes the feet of the person on his or her right. This goes on until everyone in the circle has had his or her feet washed and has washed the feet of his or her neighbour. At the end of the celebration, we all hold hands and pray the Our Father together.

I am always touched to see how different people enter into this liturgy so deeply. I am moved to see how some people who are unable to speak, who have severe handicaps and psychological problems, wash the feet of an assistant with such attentiveness and tenderness. It is normal and natural that assist- ants wash the feet of people with handicaps. There is a special beauty when a person with a handicap washes an assistant's feet. Similarly, in the Faith and Light communities of handicapped people, their parents and friends,[2] it is so beautiful to see a son or daughter with a handicap wash the feet of his or her parents.

As I became aware of the importance of this paraliturgy for L'Arche, I invited participants in L'Arche or Faith and Light retreats and other retreats to adopt the same paraliturgy. In these retreats, there are always groups of seven or eight people who meet each day to share about their faith, their love of Jesus and the gospel as well as their difficulties and their joys. During the retreat, after a talk about Jesus washing the feet of his apostles, we celebrate the paraliturgy of the washing of the feet. This creates a deep presence and communion between the people, not through words but through this gesture of love and of service. After the washing of the feet, there is a ceremony of reconciliation where those who wish can meet a priest to receive the sacrament of reconciliation or can meet a spiritual guide for a time of prayer, sharing and spiritual direction.

---

[2]   Faith and Light was founded by Marie-Hélène Mathieu and myself in 1971. A Faith and Light community consists of about thirty people: people with mental handicaps, their parents and friends. They meet together regularly and give each other support. Sometimes they spend a weekend together or take time for a retreat, a pilgrimage or a vacation group. There are now 1,300 communities throughout the world. The International Secretariat is at 3 rue de Laos, 75015 Paris.

In 1991 there was an Easter pilgrimage to Lourdes by Faith and Light. On Maundy Thursday, we performed this same paraliturgy of the washing of the feet in each of the hotels, guest houses and hospitals. The hotel owners were so touched by this that they emptied all the local stores of their jugs and basins, as they did not want their guests to lack the necessary material! In the evaluations of the pilgrimage, many mentioned the washing of the feet as one of the most significant moments, a moment of grace and of unity.

In ecumenical and inter-religious retreats in L'Arche and Faith and Light, the washing of the feet has taken on a special meaning. At these retreats, the Eucharist and the eucharistic communion cannot be the visible sign of our unity. All of us can, however, wash each other's feet. In 1995, a group of Presbyterians, Methodists, Anglicans and Roman Catholics organized a "Festival of Peace" in Northern Ireland which was like a retreat. Each day we celebrated the Eucharist according to one of the traditions, but we could not all partake of communion at the same liturgy. On the last day, in each little group that had shared together each day, we washed each other's feet. We are beginning to discover and to live the ecumenical and inter-religious dimensions of this act.

As I have become aware of how the washing of the feet touches individual hearts or affects personal relationships and community life, I have wanted to go more deeply into the mystery of this passage in the Gospel of John, and I would like to share these reflections with you.

2

THE WASHING OF THE FEET IN THE GOSPELS

A Solemn Moment

In the thirteenth chapter of his Gospel, John speaks of Jesus' descent into littleness and weakness, which will end in his condemnation and death on a cross as a blasphemer, an outcast, and a criminal. Up to this point, Jesus seemed to be so strong. He had performed miracles, healing the sick and ordering the wind and the sea to be calm, and he had spoken with authority to the scribes and Pharisees. He appeared to be a great prophet, perhaps even the Messiah. The God of power was with him. More and more people were beginning to follow him, hoping that he would drive out the Romans and thus liberate Israel and renew the dignity of the chosen people. The time of the Passover was near. The crowd and his friends were wondering: "Will he make himself known at the Passover? Then everyone will believe in him." Everyone was waiting expectantly for something special to happen. But instead of doing something extraordinary, Jesus took the downward path into weakness and seemed to allow others to triumph over him. This downward journey into weakness began when the Word became flesh in the womb of Mary. It continued in a visible way for the disciples with the washing of the feet. It will end with his agony, passion, crucifixion and death.

The beginning of the chapter is very solemn:

Now before the feast of the Passover, when Jesus knew that his hour had come to depart out of this world to the Father, having loved his own who were in the world, he loved them to the end.

And during the supper, when the devil had already put it into the heart of Judas Iscariot, Simon's son, to betray him, Jesus, knowing that the Father had given all things into his hands, and that he had come from God and was going to God, rose from supper, laid aside his garments, and girded himself with a towel.

(John 13:1-4)

These words are very moving: "Jesus, knowing that the Father had given all things into his hands, and that he had come from God and was going to

God, rose from supper, laid aside his garments . . . ."
Then he knelt down before each one of the disciples
and began washing his feet, in an attitude of
humility, submission, supplication and weakness.
On one's knees one cannot easily move nor defend
oneself.

John the Baptist had said that he was not worthy
to stoop down and untie the thongs of Jesus' sandals
(Mark 1:7). Yet here Jesus himself stoops down in
front of each one of his disciples.

The first Christians may have sung the mystery
of Jesus, who emptied himself of his glory and
descended into weakness, in the words we find in
Paul's letter to the Philippians:

> Though he was in the form of God,
> Jesus did not count equality with God a thing to
> be grasped,
> but emptied himself, taking the form of a
> servant;
> being born in the likeness of men.
> And being found in human form he humbled
> himself
> and became obedient unto death, even death on
> a cross. (Philippians 2:6-8)

We are in front of a God who becomes small and
poor, who goes down the ladder of human promotion, who takes the last place, the place of a servant

or a slave. According to Jewish custom, the slave washed the feet of his master, or sometimes wives or children washed the feet of their husband or father.

Jesus Lays Down His Garments

Jesus washes the feet of his disciples not before the meal, which could have been a Jewish custom of purification, but during the meal. Imagine the disciples' surprise when they saw Jesus get up and take off his outer garments in the middle of the Passover meal which was a particularly solemn occasion. They must have looked at each other in amazement: "What is he doing now?" It was such a strange action!

In the New Testament, we read about garments and tunics.[3] The garment is an outer gown; the tunic is a garment worn underneath. The tunic seems to have been like a long, light shirt or smock which went down to the knees and sometimes even to the ankles. The Jews wore it when they were at home in the intimacy of the family or with close friends. They put on the outer garment when they went out or when they received guests at home. Slaves did

---

[3]   All the exegetes say that Jesus wore a tunic and an outer garment or gown, but they do not agree on the exact nature (length, width, form) of either the outer garment (or coat or gown, according to different translations) or of the tunic. It is probable, too, that customs changed according to the times, to different traditions in different parts of Israel, and according to social status and position in Jewish society.

not have any outer garment; they wore only a tunic or smock.

In his account of the Passion, John says: "When the soldiers had finished crucifying Jesus, they took his clothing and divided it into four parts, one for each soldier. His undergarment (tunic) was seamless, woven in one piece from neck to hem; so they said to one another, 'Instead of tearing it, let's throw dice to decide who is to have it'" (John 19:23-24).

It seems that the soldiers tore Jesus' outer garment into four parts, in order to make dust cloths, but his tunic was too beautiful for that.

At the washing of the feet, Jesus removed his outer garment. Jesus came from Nazareth, which was known to be a village where a lot of poor people lived. His mission was to announce the Good News to the poor, to be with them and to eat with them. He had told the Twelve, when he sent them out on mission (Luke 9), not to take anything with them, not even a change of clothes, that is, not even two tunics. Jesus' own way of living was an example for his disciples of how to live simply and poorly and to be close to the poor. When he and his disciples travelled together, they often had to sleep outdoors, using their outer garment as a blanket, as many poor people did in Israel in those days. Jesus' tunic was woven in linen or cotton, in a single piece. Tunics were generally handmade by the women in a family.

Jesus' tunic was probably handwoven by Mary, his mother.

Clothing is often significant. It signifies one's position or function in life: soldiers, mayors, doctors, judges, athletes, and priests all wear clothes that reveal their function in society. Clothes often express a certain identity, dignity and authority – or lack of these – and likewise clothes can signify one's place or status in society. Rich people wear certain kinds of clothes, the poor and beggars other kinds. There are also different national dress and traditional costumes.

Perhaps Jesus had removed his outer garment for a very practical reason, so it would be easier to wash the disciples' feet. Dressed just in his tunic, he was dressed for work. But there seems to be a deeper, inner meaning to this gesture. This is indicated in John's Gospel by the way he both reveals and hides the mystery. The words he uses are: "He laid down his outer garments" and he "took them up again." These words "laid down" and "take up" are the same words Jesus uses in John 10:11,15,17, and 18 when he talks about laying down his life and taking it up again. This seems to indicate that laying down his garment means giving his life.

As Jesus removes his garments, he is stripping himself as well of any function or social status. Of course, he is Jewish and a teacher and a prophet, so he does have authority and power. But here he presents himself to his disciples just as a person, a friend. Before being Lord and teacher, he is a heart seeking to meet other hearts, a friend yearning to be in communion with friends, a loving person seeking to live in the heart of his friends.

In this domain of the heart, all people are alike. There is no visible hierarchy one could signify by dress. People with or without visible handicaps, the poor and the rich, the young and the old, people with AIDS or in good health, they all are alike and they all have the same dignity. Each one's life and history are sacred. Each person is unique and important. The only hierarchy that remains is one of love, and that remains hidden. (Is that really a hierarchy?) Each person's heart is a mystery. A man in prison may in fact be more loving than his guard or judge, a woman with a handicap more loving than her teacher, or an immigrant more loving than somebody in high office. So at the end of our lives we will be judged by how we have loved, and not by our clothes, or the masks society has imposed on us. We will be judged according to who we really are and not on our job or role in society. As Jesus removes his outer garments, he is reminding us of what is most important in life: our hearts.

Later that same night and the next morning, others will strip him of his clothes. Jesus will be tortured, condemned to death and nailed to a cross naked, like a criminal. Others will make him poor and vulnerable. He will suffer and be reduced to tears. But here, at the Last Supper, it is Jesus himself who removes his own garments.

We could say, and this seems to be the meaning of Paul's words in Philippians, that in this way Jesus, who is the Word of God, the only Beloved Son of the Father, hides his glory by taking the downward path of humility and littleness. Perhaps it would be more exact, however, to say that he is in fact revealing his true glory, his true nature, the deepest meaning of his being and the most intimate desires of his heart. God is love and wants to give life to others by drawing them into the heart and the love of the Trinity.

The Holy Spirit throughout the Old Testament, and Jesus himself in the Gospels, often repeats, "Be not afraid." It is as if God's great concern is that we not be frightened of him, that we not see God only as a Law-giver, a superior distant Being to whom we owe honour and glory. It is true, God is a superior Being, a Law-giver as well as a mother, father or source of life for all of creation. There is a huge gap between the infinite, transcendent, immortal God and the limits and mortality of our humanity. But the Word became flesh in Mary's womb in order to bridge this gap and to reveal God as a friend, a lover, the Beloved of all humanity, who invites each person to participate in the communion, compassion and ecstasy he lives with the Father at the heart of the Trinity. He wants to invite us all to the divine Wedding Feast.

Later that evening Jesus tells his disciples: "I do not call you servants any longer, but I call you friends" (John 15:14). Friendship means equality and openness; it implies a certain inter-dependence. Jesus says: "Ask what you will, and it shall be done unto you" (John 15:7). Isn't that the attitude of a friend who is open and ready to do anything a friend may ask? Isn't that the gift Jesus wants to give to each one of us?

By laying aside his outer garments, Jesus signifies that he is putting aside all that could be an obstacle to a communion of hearts.

Jesus Washes His Disciples' Feet

"He girded himself with a towel. Then he poured water into a basin, and began to wash the disciples' feet, and to wipe them with the towel which he had tied around him" (John 13:4-5). The disciples resist. Peter reacts strongly. He expresses what is probably in the heart of each of the disciples. This same resistance is perhaps in each one of us. What would we say if Jesus, our Lord, appeared before us and started to wash our dirty clothes or to clean the house? Wouldn't we be embarrassed and shocked? Wouldn't we tell Jesus to go and sit down in the living room and that we would serve him whatever he wants?

He came to Simon Peter who said to him: "Lord, are you going to wash my feet?" Jesus answered: "You do not know now what I am doing, but later you will understand." Peter said to him: "You shall never wash my feet." Jesus answered: "Unless I wash you, you have no share with me." (John 13:6-9)

Even though Jesus takes a humble, submissive position in front of Peter, he maintains his authority. He speaks clearly and forcefully: "If I do not wash you, you have no part in me." These are powerful words which in simple language mean: "If I cannot wash your feet, you will no longer be my friend, my disciple. You cannot enter into my kingdom and receive my heritage. Everything is finished between us, you can leave now." To have one's feet washed by Jesus is not optional; it is an essential condition for becoming his friend and entering into his kingdom of love. Peter cannot understand.

Peter realizes the sternness and the gravity of Jesus' answer and he is shaken. Perhaps it reminds him of Jesus' words after Jesus had called him "the rock" on which the church would be built and he had reproached Jesus for announcing his suffering and death. Jesus replied: "Get behind me, Satan! You are setting a stumbling block for me; for your mind is not on divine things but on human things!" (Matthew 16:23). Harsh words! Why did Jesus respond so strongly? This harshness hides an urgency and a great vulnerability. Jesus is vulnerable. To accept to go down a path of pain and suffering, to give one's life, to accept to become humble, like a slave, without rights, to take the last place: all this goes against the normal desires in the human heart. Our desire is to be someone, to show who one is through our origins, qualities, capacities and basic rights. To be willing to give up these things is not easy for Jesus, for Jesus remains a human being, like us in all things except sin. This is, however, the path of love linked to pain that is given to him by the Father, a path on which he will live a total communion with the Father and reveal his radical love for his friends "to the end." It is urgent that Peter understand.

In front of the unexpected strength and sternness of Jesus' response, "If I do not wash you, you have no part in me," Peter gives in. He opens up to Jesus, without understanding, because he could not bear being separated from Jesus. So he cries out, "Lord, not my feet only but also my hands and my head!" Perhaps he thinks that Jesus is creating a new purification ritual. But Jesus affirms that it is not that: "He who has bathed does not need to wash, except for his feet,[4] but he is clean all over; and you are clean, but not all of you." For he knew who was to

_____

[4] These words "except for his feet" are present in some older texts and absent in others. They might refer to a Jewish custom in preparation for a feast. Each person was to bathe and dress especially for the celebration. But just before the meal, they were to wash their feet.

betray him; that was why he said, "You are not all clean" (John 13:10-11).

"You Should Do As I Have Done to You"

When he had washed their feet, and taken his garments, and resumed his place, he said to them: "Do you know what I have done to you? You call me Teacher and Lord; and you are right, for so I am. If I then, your Lord and Teacher, have washed your feet, you also ought to wash one another's feet. For I have given you an example, that you also should do as I have done to you. Truly, truly, I say to you, a servant is not greater than his master; nor is he who is sent greater than he who sent him. If you know these things, blessed are you if you do them."

(John 13:12-17)

If Jesus washes his disciples' feet, he wants to signify his love for each one and to show each one that humility and service are the key to his message. Peter reacts rather violently to Jesus kneeling humbly before him: "You shall never wash my feet!"

Jesus insists that they should not only let him wash their feet, but that they too ought to wash each other's feet. He is giving an example. So, just as it is not optional to have Jesus wash their feet, so too it is not optional for the disciples to wash each other's feet.

Note that this is the only place in the Gospels where Jesus says: "I have given you an example." Jesus is our model. In other places he asks us to learn from him or to do certain things he has done. Here he insists that if we want to be his disciples, to be part of his kingdom, we have to follow his example and wash each other's feet. We have to do things that seem to go beyond common sense and against our habits, customs and cultural traditions.

Of course, Jesus is asking us above all to have a certain attitude towards others. It is not just a question of washing feet. The washing of the feet is a sign and a symbol. Jesus is asking us to live and act constantly with a humble and loving heart in regard to others. But at the same time, Jesus insists on the importance of washing, of touching each other's feet.

In the following chapters we will look further at the meaning of this gesture, for each disciple of Jesus is invited to enter more deeply into this mystery, in and through a new gift of the Holy Spirit, and to discover its meaning.

Jesus Proclaims a New Beatitude

After insisting that the apostles wash each other's feet, Jesus affirms that if they do, they will be blessed: "If you know these things, blessed are you if you do them" (John 13:17).

The beatitudes are at the heart of Jesus' message. They are the foundation of all his teaching, and the charter for all Christians. At the same time, the beatitudes are a gift of God. They put people into a new relationship with God. In the Gospels there are the well-known "official" beatitudes in Matthew and Luke, but there are other, more hidden beatitudes throughout the Gospels.

- Blessed are the poor in spirit, for theirs is the kingdom of heaven.
- Blessed are those who mourn, for they shall be comforted.
- Blessed are the meek, for they shall inherit the earth.
- Blessed are those who hunger and thirst for righteousness, for they shall be satisfied.
- Blessed are the merciful, for they shall obtain mercy.
- Blessed are the pure of heart, for they shall see God.
- Blessed are the peacemakers, for they shall be called sons and daughters of God.
- Blessed are those who are persecuted for righteousness' sake, for theirs is the kingdom of heaven.

Blessed are you when people revile you and persecute you and utter all kinds of evil against you falsely on my account. Rejoice and be glad, for your reward is great in heaven, for so people persecuted the prophets who were before you.

(Matthew 5:3-12)

Blessed are you, the poor, for yours is the kingdom of God.

Blessed are you who hunger now, for you shall be filled.

Blessed are you who weep now, for you shall laugh.

Blessed are you when people hate you, and when they separate you from their company and shall reproach you, and cast out your name as evil, for the Son of man's sake. Rejoice in that day and leap for joy; for behold, your reward is great in heaven: for in like manner did their fathers unto the prophets. (Luke 6:20-26)

Then there are the more hidden beatitudes: Blessed are those who eat with the poor (Luke 14); Blessed are those who believe without seeing (John 20:29); Blessed are those who listen to the word of God and put it into practice (Luke 11:28); Elizabeth proclaimed Mary "blessed" (Luke 1:42-43); and in her Magnificat, Mary herself says that "all generations shall call me blessed." And then there is the blessedness of washing each other's feet.

In the original Jerusalem Bible, the Greek word for "beatitude" was translated by "happy." That is not wrong, if we understand the deepest meaning of happiness. For it is truly a joy to wash the feet of the poor and the weak, to live in communion with them. There is a deep, but often hidden joy, in being united to Jesus in his pain, tears and rejection; to know that he is with us in it all. There is also an inner joy in discovering the meaning of all our suffering.

The new Jerusalem Bible, along with most modern translations, goes back to the word "blessed," which is perhaps more correct since it carries with it that sense of a deeper inner joy than is signified by the word "happy." "Blessed are you if you wash your brothers' and sisters' feet." "Blessed are you if you live in a spirit of poverty; God is close to you." It is truly a blessing to live as Jesus lived. God is close to those who wash others' feet and who eat at the table of the poor, the lame, the crippled and the blind. God watches over them, protects them, and gives them new strength. Even more than that: God lives in them. They become like Jesus. They have been "clothed in Christ" (Galatians 3:27). They have put on a "new self," become a "new creation" (Colossians 3:10; Ephesians 4:24). That is the joy and that is the sign of God's presence on earth.

So the beatitudes are a new gift of the Holy Spirit. On a purely human level, it is impossible to live them. In fact, they appear quite absurd. The beatitudes flow from a real presence of God within us and they lead us into a new relationship with God.

The Washing of the Feet and the Eucharist

John does not mention the institution of the Eucharist at the Last Supper, but only the washing of the feet. This is quite surprising, as John gives such prominence to Jesus' words about the bread of life and the gift of his body and blood (John 6). Perhaps our reflections in this book show how complementary these two actions are. You cannot understand the one without the other. One necessarily leads to the other and one without the other would be a distortion of what Jesus envisioned.

After the institution of the Eucharist at the Last Supper, Jesus said, "Do this in memory of me." After the washing of the feet he said: "I have given you an example so that you also may do what I have done for you." As we have already said, this is the only time in all of the Gospels that Jesus tells his disciples, "I have given you an example." I am a model for you.

Jesus performs these two symbolic acts just before his death. After a few intimate words to his disciples, he leaves for Gethsemane, where he will endure agony and then be arrested. The soldiers will bring him to the High Priest. That same afternoon, he will be dead. These last two actions are his final testimony.

These two symbolic acts around the body, his own body and the body of each one of his disciples, are gestures of communion and love. In both of them Jesus is not teaching or giving something to his disciples; he is giving himself.

There is a great gentleness and tenderness in these two gestures. Jesus wants to be with his followers, for he loves them and wants to live in them. He does not want to dominate or control them. On the contrary, he makes himself little and humble. He lets himself be eaten by them in the Eucharist and he takes the place of a slave or of a child in the footwashing. In so doing, he reveals to us a God hidden in littleness.

These two actions are linked: in order to wash others' feet, that is, in order to be as humble and loving as Jesus, we need to be nourished by his body and blood in the Eucharist. Without this presence of Jesus in us, it is impossible to live out such poverty and such humility; without the Eucharist we cannot live out such a deep presence and communion of the heart with others. On the other hand, we cannot adequately receive the body and blood of Jesus unless we are forgiving and loving towards others.

3

THE SIGNIFICANCE OF THE WASHING OF THE FEET

A Symbol and a Prophecy of Life in the Kingdom

If Jesus washes his disciples' feet, it is not just to give them a lesson in humility which they could have understood, even if it might be difficult to accept. Jesus says to Peter: "Later on you will understand." The washing of the feet is a mystery which we can only enter through a gift of the Holy Spirit. Peter will receive this gift at Pentecost. Jesus brings a whole new vision, a whole new way of living, which is impossible if we rely on our own human resources. The washing of the feet summarizes the teaching and the message of Jesus. Actions speak louder than words.

At that time the disciples came to Jesus saying: "Who is the greatest in the kingdom of heaven?"

And calling to him a child, he put him in the midst of them and said: "Truly I say to you, unless you turn and become like children, you will never enter the kingdom of heaven. Whoever humbles himself like this child, he is the greatest in the kingdom of heaven."

(Matthew 18:1-4)

"The kings of the Gentiles exercise lordship over them; and those in authority are called benefactors. But this must not be so with you; rather let the greatest among you become as the youngest, and the leader as one who serves. For which is the greater, the one who sits at table, or the one who serves? Is it not the one who sits at table? But I am among you as one who serves."

(Luke 22:25-27)

Jesus realizes that his disciples will always be tempted to imitate the "kings of the Gentiles," to go along with the values of the surrounding culture; to exercise authority and help the poor from "on top," as someone superior, out of pity or even a certain disdain. His kingdom, however, is completely different, unlike any other kingdom. In his kingdom, the greatest become, or rather are, the smallest and the leader becomes (is) a servant. For it is a kingdom of love, a kingdom where the weakest and the most humble are given the most prominent place. This kingdom is a body, where each member has a place and no one is excluded; each one is a sign of love. In his kingdom, the smallest and the poorest both attract and radiate love.

The kingdom Jesus describes, of course, is Heaven, which is the fullness of life, where we will live fully in God and with God. In Heaven there will be no more pain or sin or evil or tears, for God, ecstasy in God, will be "all in all." Each person will be moved and inspired by divine ecstasy and live in the fullness of light and of love.

Jesus affirms, however, that this kingdom has already come and is present here and now on this earth. In Luke's text of the beatitudes Jesus is providing the fundamental orientation for his disciples and for the Church on earth. We have difficulty recognizing this kingdom of God because it is so small and hidden, like treasure hidden in a field. We human beings are so attracted by power and glory that frequently we do not see it, or want to see it.

In order to show the radical newness of life in his kingdom, Jesus washes the feet of his disciples. This shocks and scandalizes them. They find this gesture unacceptable, they cannot understand, and so this becomes a moment of painful testing for them. Jesus, their Lord and Teacher, kneels down in front of each one, as if in a relation of submission and obedience to them. No culture would permit such a thing. In every culture the boss is the boss! A superior is always superior, inevitably "on top"! But it's as if Jesus is trying to say: "Yes, this is the way to love in my kingdom." That is why to have one's feet washed by Jesus is not something optional, but a vital, necessary part of discipleship. It means entering into a whole new world.

The folly of his action illustrates and prepares for another folly: Jesus stripped of his clothes, totally naked, nailed to a cross, crying out "I thirst," and, "My God, my God, why have you abandoned me?" Jesus identifies himself not only with the slave, but with a criminal, with all those who feel themselves to be totally abandoned by God. In and through the weakness of the cross, in his acceptance of total defeat, Jesus gives life to the world and saves all of humanity. By taking the violence of humanity into his own flesh, he transforms it into tenderness and forgiveness. He opens the door to divine love for all humankind. Isn't that what Paul means when he says that "God's folly is wiser than human wisdom, and that God's weakness is stronger than human strength" (1 Corinthians 1:25)?

Isaiah announces this folly (Isaiah 53) when he speaks of the man of sorrows, with no beauty in him, so disfigured that he no longer looked like a human being; he was despised and rejected by all. But, says Isaiah, and this is the folly of God: he was bearing our suffering, carrying our sorrows, he was wounded and crushed because of our faults. His disfigured face has rendered our faces more human, more compassionate. We have been healed by his wounds. Jesus is not giving a lesson on authority, but revealing the ways of his kingdom, showing us who he really is and how God loves "to the very end."

Jesus goes even further into this folly of weakness and love. He calls his disciples not only to announce a God who is weak and who is foolish in the eyes of human beings, but also to follow his example: to love others "to the end." Jesus is the model. He calls his friends to follow him on this road of love, through apparently foolish, scandalous gestures.

A Communion of Love with Each Person

Jesus had already had his own feet washed by a woman's tears (Luke 7:36) and by the precious nard or perfumed ointment of Mary of Bethany (John 12). He must have felt in his own heart all the love contained in this gesture and been moved by this expression of love and the relationship it established. He wanted to express his love for his disciples in the same way. Through words he had communicated with the disciples as a community. Now, through this intimate action, he affirms a personal relationship with each one. As he knelt down, he must have looked at each one with such gentleness and love, calling him by name. At the same time this gesture is a "good-bye." Jesus knows that the next day he will be put to death; this is the last time he will touch his friends. He must have touched the feet of each one so gently, with such affection, with all the fire of the love and the humility which unite him to his Father.

Being so vulnerable and sensitive, Jesus perhaps had to do this not only to express his love, but to communicate the communion he has with his Father, and that he yearns to live with his disciples.

Even though the disciples do not understand, and Peter's reticence is proof of their lack of understanding, each one lets Jesus wash his feet. Each permits Jesus' love to become communion, in other words, for love to be given and received, for love to be shared. To remove one's shoes before another person already expresses a certain intimacy with that person, doesn't it? Isn't that the meaning of God's words to Moses: "Take off your shoes, for the ground you are standing on is holy ground" (Exodus 3:5)? With the Word becoming flesh, the new "holy ground" is the body of Jesus. Through the gift of the Holy Spirit, each person's body becomes "holy ground," the new temple of God.

The way Jesus touched his disciples must have made them understand, even if only later, the sacredness of their own bodies. The body is the place where the Father dwells.

The friendship and relationship contained in washing feet, the way it communicates love, were revealed to me in a special way when I lived my sabbatical year in "La Forestière," one of our L'Arche homes that welcomes ten men and women with severe handicaps. None of these people can speak and most cannot walk or eat by themselves. Each one has felt abandoned. What is important is to reveal to them their value and beauty, to help transform the negative image they have of themselves into a positive one and to communicate to them a desire to live. This communication is essentially through touch, presence and a non-verbal language. One of the most meaningful moments of the day in La Forestière is bath time, a time of relationship, when by the way we touch and bathe each person we can help each one become aware of his or her own beauty and value. Words are, of course, absolutely vital in some situations as they explain what is being done and affirm the meaning of certain actions, but the gesture itself is of vital importance.

When love is given and received, a trust and peace enters the heart which the face and the whole body radiate. A few years ago Peter arrived in L'Arche. He was quite a difficult man who absolutely refused to communicate with anyone. He was completely closed up in himself with delinquent tendencies. One day we discovered that he had athlete's foot. The doctor prescribed some medication and asked us to wash his feet three times a day. From the day we started to touch and bathe his feet,

Peter began to open up. His whole attitude towards us changed. This showed us once again the importance of the washing of the feet

While I was living at La Forestière, I became more aware of the importance of Paul's words: "Do you not realize that you are a temple of the Holy Spirit, who is in you and whom you received from God in you? . . . So use your body for the glory of God" (1 Corinthians 6:19).

If the body is truly the dwelling-place of God, a holy ground, then all our relationships are transformed. When we meet and touch others, we do so with even more respect as we realize their life is holy. When Jesus washes his disciples' feet and asks us to do the same, is he not showing us the importance of meeting each other, touching each other, with simplicity, gentleness and great respect, because each person is precious?

Forgiveness That Gives Life

In Holy Scripture, water signifies life and forgiveness. Water cleanses, purifies, refreshes, gives life. No water means no life. The earth becomes a desert; there is death.

To forgive means to give life, to remove what has been an obstacle to friendship and communion: those inner, psychological walls that had prevented dialogue or communication. These walls are judgements that separate and isolate us from others and push people into anguish and inner death. To forgive means we no longer judge others. Forgiveness breaks down blockages to communication and communion so that we can say to another: "I appreciate you just as you are; I love you and want you to live." Isn't the washing of the feet a prefiguration of the sacrament of reconciliation and the power that Jesus gives to priests to forgive sins?

John the Baptist invited people to be purified and baptized in the waters of the Jordan. Jesus inaugurated a baptism of water *and* the Holy Spirit. He declared that people had to be reborn, transformed, by the waters that communicate the Holy Spirit (John 3). As Jesus humbly kneels before each of his disciples and washes their feet, he forgives them from below. He does not forgive them from on high, like a master or superior. The disciples have trouble understanding Jesus. They are too closed up in their own idea of the Messiah, what he should be like and what he should do. They wanted to have a prominent place with him and they often argued over who was the most important among themselves. Jesus knows them and is well aware of their fears, their wounds, their defence mechanisms and their need to prove themselves and to be seen as important. He washes the dirt from their feet as a sign that he takes away the dirt in their hearts. Jesus washes Peter's feet, forgiving him in advance, knowing that later on Peter will disown him.

Feet are a symbol of authority and sometimes even of hardness. In some cultures, people kiss the feet of another as a sign of respect for that person and of obedience to him or her. Here Jesus cleanses the disciples of their abuse of authority and purifies them of their desires for power and greatness.

St. Bernard says that "feet represent the yearnings and desires of the soul," that is, tenderness and love. He affirms that the "sacrament of the washing of the feet" signifies a forgiveness with regard to all our daily sins.[5] We are all deeply wounded in our capacity for relationship and love; we are so frightened of others, and especially frightened of difference. How quickly we try to control others and thus wound them and crush their freedom. Here, Jesus forgives his friends all their lack of compassion, kindness and love in regard to others.

When Jesus washes the feet of Judas, he knows that Judas will soon betray him, and that, in doing so, Judas will be betraying the deepest part of his own being. Jesus loves Judas whom he had called to follow him and to be his friend. But he does not try to stop Judas; through this gesture he simply says: "I love you. No matter what happens I will still love you. I know your fragility, your wounds and the

---

[5]   "Do you want to know why this act of Jesus has the value of a sacrament and not just an example? Pay attention to his words to Peter: 'If I do not wash your feet you will have no part with me' (John 13:8). Something essential to our salvation must be hidden in this act" (St. Bernard, Sermon for Holy Thursday).

jealousy in your heart. I know that the devil is trying to get you. But I love you and, oh, how I yearn for you to be fully alive and loving, free of all fear and free especially of the evil spirit." When Judas hangs himself from a tree and the noose of the rope tightens around his neck, during those last moments of asphyxiation, perhaps Judas remembered Jesus' face and eyes which had filled with love as he washed his feet. Perhaps Judas' eyes then filled with tears as he received the forgiveness of Jesus.

To Exercise Authority Humbly, as a Service

The word "authority" comes from the Latin "augere" (to grow). All authority, whether it be civil, parental, religious or community, is intended to help people grow towards greater freedom, justice and truth. Often, however, it is used for the honour, power, privilege, and positive self-image of those who exercise it. By stooping down to wash the disciples' feet, Jesus calls us all to exercise authority humbly, as a service.

Some children have never known parental love. They had authoritarian fathers who wanted to control everything, who did not understand or affirm them. Or perhaps their fathers were absent, not interested in what they did. Maybe their mothers were depressed or possessive, trying to keep them from growing up so that they would need them and stay attached to them. Or else conflicts between parents created a sense of insecurity and an ambivalent attitude in regard to authority. Authority is then seen as harmful and crushing one's freedom. Children are lost in front of an authority that does not give security, which is not concerned with their growth, freedom and happiness. In order to live and grow harmoniously, children need an authority that loves and respects them, that gives clear guidelines and a deep sense of security. When children have had a bad experience with authority, they will have difficulty taking on responsibility and exercising authority when they themselves become adults. They have never had good models.

Sometimes authority becomes mere power. When we are given authority, we start organizing everything and everyone; we no longer care for people, especially for those who are in the minority or marginalized. We often try to control others and stifle their freedom. We start finding pleasure in having power and in all the privileges that are attached to a function. Then we tend not to listen to those who disturb us and whose criticisms and anger reveal our mistakes.

The need for power can often hide and compensate for a lack of inner strength. Due to a certain vulnerability and inner weakness we over-identify with our position. *If we lose it or if we no longer have power, it is as if we no longer exist.* We need to feel superior and look at others as subordinates.

Then we hide behind our role instead of becoming a good shepherd who serves others and the common good.

In Chapter 10 of John's Gospel, Jesus describes the qualities of good shepherds. Good shepherds know their sheep by name. To know someone's name is to know his or her gifts, qualities and inner wounds as well as his or her vocation and mission in life. This requires listening to each one attentively. The good shepherd walks ahead of the flock, knowing what direction to take. Because the sheep know their shepherd, they trust and follow him or her. When a wolf comes, in other words, when there is danger, the shepherd will defend them. Good shepherds are not afraid to enter into conflict and to risk their lives for the sheep, to sacrifice their own interests in order to love. The sheep feel secure and sense that they are loved to the end.

When Jesus speaks of the good shepherd, he is describing himself, but he is also reminding us of what is essential in the exercise of all authority, so that it be constructive and not destructive. Jesus invites all of us to be good shepherds. He calls us all to live responsibly in a spirit of service, with humility, to help others grow spiritually and humanly, whether as parents, business leaders, heads of government, army officers, priests, teachers, or assistants in L'Arche. And he promises to give us the grace, the strength and the love to do it.

Authority Become Communion

By washing his disciples' feet, however, Jesus is calling them not just to be good shepherds, but to exercise authority at the heart of community in a totally new way, a way that is humanly incomprehensible and impossible. It is just as new and just as impossible as his invitation to forgive seventy-times-seven times, to love enemies and to do good to those who hate us, to give our clothes to those who ask for them, to be constantly gentle and non-violent. It is just as amazing as when he identifies himself with the poor and the outcast. "In my kingdom, the greatest must become the smallest." Jesus asks his disciples to exercise authority like a child or a servant, where they are vulnerable and open to others. Can this authority "from below," where, out of love, we place ourselves lower than others, still be called authority? Is it not rather love and communion? It is like the authority a child has over a mother, or a friend over a friend, or a wife over her husband and vice versa. They are there for one another, at each other's service. They listen to one another and are never too busy to be disturbed by the other. They live inside one another. Their joy is in giving to each other and being in communion one with another.

But how to move from exercising authority from "on high," from a place of superiority, to exercising authority from "below"? Will we not lose the security of being the "boss" who has firm beliefs, knows everything, plans well and is in control? Won't this insecurity bring a feeling of emptiness and anguish? Don't we have to leave our human ways of doing things in order to do things as God does them? This emptiness or poverty of spirit becomes then the place where the Holy Spirit can take over, enter into us, guide us, and give us new strength. Isn't this like the grain of wheat that must die in order to bear fruit? Isn't this what it means to pass through the dark night of the soul in order to reach the light?

Jesus is affirming his friends by this act of love, encouraging them to have confidence in themselves and in their mission in life. He washes their feet and sends them out barefoot, to walk the paths that the Holy Spirit will show them, so that they may become in their own flesh the Good News of love as well as proclaiming it through their word. Soon Jesus will no longer be with them; he will leave the world. They, as friends of Jesus, will continue to spread his message and be his presence in the world, through the gift of the Spirit that he and the Father will send them. And they must go in total poverty, "on foot," and do the impossible:

He called the twelve together and gave them
power and authority
over all devils and to cure diseases,
and he sent them out to proclaim the kingdom of
God and to heal.
He said to them: "Take nothing for the journey:
neither staff, nor bag, nor bread, nor money,
and do not have a spare tunic."

(Luke 9:1-3)

If they are called to live in poverty and insecurity, to do what is humanly impossible, it is because
the Father will take care of them and watch over
them. The Father will send them the strength they
need; He will give them the Holy Spirit. As he
washes their feet, Jesus is telling them: "You must
live as I have lived, as a poor person and as a
beloved of the Father. Do not seek honours or privileges; seek only to serve others gently and humbly,
to be an instrument of my love and of my word. And
I will be with you every day, inspiring you, giving
you the necessary words and strength."

Jesus lives his authority in total communion
with the Father, as a child of the Father. He never
tried to prove who he was or what he could do.
Everything he did and said was in union with the
Father, in order to glorify the Father. Jesus exercises
authority out of love and for love, to communicate
love. And now, Jesus' followers, like little children,

are called to do everything in communion with Jesus. They will speak Jesus' words. They will wash each other's feet. They will communicate his love. They will be Jesus.

L'Arche's mission is to welcome people with mental handicaps, to help them discover their beauty and the meaning of their lives. Assistants need to help them grow and find new life humanly as well as spiritually. We have discovered two different ways of exercising authority, from "on top" and from "below." Sometimes it is necessary to give orders and clear instructions, to teach, to organize, to show the way with firmness. That is exercising authority from "on top." Most of the time in L'Arche, however, we need to call others to life, to help them stand up on their own feet, to help them trust in themselves and their own inner capacity for love. This is done through our love and compassion; by meeting them where they are, in a heart-to-heart relationship.

During Jesus' public life he often taught others and performed miracles with great force and assurance. Even the winds and the sea obeyed him. When he is at his disciples' feet, however, he is no longer giving orders or teaching; he is helping them to discover their value and mission. Jesus does not deny or disown the authority he had during his public life. He calls his disciples to teach and to exercise their authority with the same clarity and firmness. But here, at their feet, he is showing them another path, the path of love, of trust and of communion which is the sign of the kingdom and which calls for a new humility and poverty.

Going Down to Meet God[6]

As he wraps the towel around him and stoops down in front of each disciple, Jesus is living out what he had announced a few weeks earlier:

Be like people waiting for their master to return from the wedding feast,
ready to open the door as soon as he comes and knocks.
Blessed those servants whom the master finds awake when he comes.
In truth I tell you, he will do up his belt,
sit them down at table
and wait on them. (Luke 12:35-37)

Everything is turned upside down! Instead of serving the head of the house, it is the head of the house who serves the others! This is the logic of love, the logic of a God who takes the downward path and goes lower and lower; a God who empties himself and is humiliated (cf. Philippians 2). Let us try to understand this logic of love.

---

[6] This is the title of a book by Benjamin Gonzalez Buelta, S.J., in the collection "Vie Chrétienne," No. 395, Paris.

As we said earlier, by removing his garments Jesus is revealing his true glory, his deepest self, his heart's most intimate desire. He becomes smaller and smaller, more and more vulnerable, in order to communicate love. Often we admire people who are important, but we are also a bit frightened of them. We are drawn to love someone who seems little and who needs us. That is where the mystery of Jesus lies: he becomes small and humble in order to live with the disciples the same union and communion he lives with His Father. Jesus is reminding us that from now on he is hidden in the poor, that if we want to find him and to meet him, we must come closer to the poor.

After this gesture of love and compassion towards his disciples, Jesus becomes even poorer: the man of compassion becomes a man in need of compassion; the man who had told all those who thirst to come to him to drink, will cry out on the cross, "I thirst." The all-powerful one becomes powerless.

By becoming a servant and a slave and washing others' feet, Jesus is identifying himself with the poor and the powerless, as he had identified himself with those who are sick, hungry, thirsty, strangers, naked, or in prison (cf. Matthew 25). It is the same mystery he is revealing: God is not only close to those who are humble, lonely and in pain, but he is hidden in them. They are no longer seen as useless, on the bottom of the ladder of human promotion; they are now a presence of God.

One day the apostles tried to prevent children from coming close to Jesus. He became angry: "Let the little children come to me, do not stop them! For it is to such as these that the kingdom of God belongs. In truth I tell you, anyone who does not welcome the kingdom of God like a little child will never enter it" (Mark 10:14-15). And another time, he took a child in his arms and said: "Anyone who welcomes this little child in my name welcomes me; and anyone who welcomes me, welcomes the one who sent me" (Luke 9:48).

In the parable of the wedding feast (Luke 14), Jesus affirms that many good, healthy people, people who no doubt were virtuous and had a good place in society, were invited but refused the invitation. And so it was that the invitation went out to people who were poor, weak, crippled, lame and blind, people with all kinds of handicaps, and they all accepted and filled the room! The life and teachings of Jesus turn everything upside down. Those closest to God now are the humble and the weak, no longer those in power, sitting on their thrones. This is God's new vision for society and for humanity. Certainly, if leaders are poor enough, they are close to God. But with Jesus we are all invited to discover how the poor and the outcast are a presence of God.

As Jesus stoops down in front of his disciples, he is telling us not to seek the best place, but to be part of a community, a "body" where the poor and the weak are held in honour.

"When you are a guest, make your way to the lowest place and sit there. . . . For everyone who raises himself up will be humbled, and the one who humbles himself will be raised up" (Luke 14:10, 11).

When Jesus calls his disciples to take the lowest place, he is not just inviting them to be humble and small in order to fight against pride and the need to be important. Ben Sirac had already taught that in Ecclesiasticus:

My child, be gentle in carrying out your business,
and you will be better loved than a lavish giver.
The greater you are, the more humbly you should behave,
and then you will find favour with the Lord;
for great though the power of the Lord is,
he accepts the homage of the humble.
(Ecclesiasticus 3:17-21)

Jesus tells us that by taking the lowest place we will meet the poor, the weak, the crippled, the blind and the outcast, who are all signs of the presence of God. As we become their friends, we become friends of God. Jesus does not oblige us to accept this new vision. He does not set up a series of rules and regulations so that we follow what he says. He simply invites each one, rich or poor, to take this downward path. It is a path that brings new poverty and sometimes anguish, but it is a path of deep liberation, reconciliation, peace and joy.

4

THE WASHING OF THE FEET:
A CALL TO UNITY

Divisions between Groups and within the Group

By kneeling down before each one, Jesus is saying that he came to destroy prejudice and the walls that separate human beings; he yearns to gather together into one body all the scattered children of God. There is no longer any elite, some who are "superior," better than others, separated and protected by a wall from those who are no good. All are beloved friends.

In our world there are all the divisions of race, religion, and culture. There are also all the divisions within the same culture: divisions around social standing, education, gender, and competence.

Ethnic groups so easily close up in themselves, each group thinking it is the best, the elite and especially chosen by God. If they have power, they try to impose their ways on others; the members of such elite groups are frightened of anyone who is different. The movement of people throughout the world and throughout history, the various invasions, colonisations and migrations, the movement of refugees, have brought a real mixture of peoples and cultures. In big cities throughout the world, there is now a pluralism: people of various cultural and religious backgrounds meet, work and live together daily. Traditional values have lost their importance and an entirely materialistic and economic culture has arisen, which tends to eliminate all ethnic differences.

However, another phenomenon has reappeared in recent years: ethnic cleansing. There is a fear of foreigners, a growing intolerance, a desire to get rid of those who are different and who present an obstacle to cultural unity. This desire sometimes seems stronger than the search for economic unity. The search for cultural unity and a common identity is important for human growth. But there is always the danger that it will lead to other Auschwitz concentration camps, other Bosnias, other Rwandas, to other tribal and inter-religious wars.

Divisions within the same society are often based on wealth, social standing, gender, or capabilities. The powerful tend to despise and exploit the weak. People with mental handicaps are put away, hidden, and locked up in institutions. Or else special facilities created for them begin to cost too much and so people are encouraged to eliminate them before birth. They are seen as "useless"; they "eat up" too much of our economic and human resources.

People can justify this vision of society which is like a pyramid. They say it is normal that people who are competent and have power, such as teachers, intellectuals and wealthy owners, be "on top" and that those who are less competent, manual labourers, immigrants and so on, should be on the bottom. Those on top are seen as being close to Almighty God, capable of exercising great virtues of justice and of seeking the truth. Those on the bottom are seen as closer to matter, taken up with material tasks, with little or no time for things of the mind and spirit. On the religious level they are often regarded as living more from superstition and myths. And on the very bottom of the social ladder there are all the unemployed, people with handicaps, and especially those with mental handicaps. Good leaders, on top of the pyramid, should certainly be concerned about the plight of each person. They are there to help each one find his or her place and be as happy as possible. This vision corresponds more or less to that of Aristotle and Plato and there is some truth to it. People should live according to the gifts and capacities that God has given them.

This vision, however, is so often perverted, with those "on top" crushing those "on the bottom": exploiting them, oppressing them, keeping them poor, refusing them higher education, depriving them of their basic rights and a fully human life. Pyramidal societies become places of harsh competition and struggle where each person tries to have more money, more influence, more power. Everyone has to win, whether it be at work, in school, in sports, or even in relationships. And for every person who wins and who climbs up the social ladder, many more lose and fall down into the pits of depression, discouragement, unemployment, anger and revolt.

Jesus came to change this type of society into a body where each person has his or her place.

Each Person, Each Group Thinks, "We Are the Best"

We human beings are so wounded and broken in our hearts and in our capacity for relationship. How quickly we try to avoid others, because we feel inferior and depressed, or else we are aggressive towards them, judging, blaming or devaluating them.

In other books[7] I have written more about the way our hearts have been wounded in our early childhood, when we felt rejected, not loved as unique by our parents. This initial wound is difficult to bear; it provokes anguish, guilt and sometimes a desire for vengeance. At a very young age, a child discovers the pain caused by the breakdown of love and trust. So he sets up defence systems to protect himself from all the pain, but also from love and communion which can also appear to be potentially dangerous. And so the child takes another path which deviates more and more from the path of love and communion. As he grows up he seeks to prove himself and to be unique through power, the admiration of others, dreams and distractions. Anguish becomes a source of energy propelling him to succeed, to be independent, to seek recognition, and to flee from any source of humiliation and depreciation. Thus, he enters into competition with others, wanting to be first, to climb the ladder. This implies a struggle and even a certain violence between competitors.

The apostles themselves did not escape from this need to be more important than the others. As soon as Jesus turned his back, they argued about

---

[7]   *Man and Woman He Made Them*, U.S.A.: Paulist Press; London: Darton, Longman and Todd; and *Toute personne est une histoire sacrée*, Paris: Plon.

which one was the best, the most loved by Jesus, the one who had best understood Jesus:

> They came to Capernaum, and when he got into the house he asked them:
> "What were you arguing about on the road?"
> They said nothing, because on the road they had been arguing
> which of them was the greatest.
> So he sat down, called the twelve to him and said:
> "If anyone wants to be first, he must make himself last of all
> and servant of all."
> He then took a little child whom he set among them and embraced,
> and he said to them: "Anyone who welcomes a little child such as this in my name, welcomes me; and anyone who welcomes me,
> welcomes not me but the one who sent me."
>
> (Mark 9:33-37)

Jesus Calls Us to Unity in One Body

Jesus yearns to meet each one of us, personally, in a heart-to-heart relationship, above and beyond the barriers or defence mechanisms that might exist. He wants to reveal to us how much we are loved, that we are truly a beloved son or daughter of the Father, that there is no longer any need to prove ourselves, to seek success or recognition in order to have value. That is the Good News! Each one of us can discover for ourselves, in our deepest self, what the prophet Isaiah announces to the people of Israel in the name of God:

Do not be afraid, for I have redeemed you;
I have called you by your name, you are mine.
Should you pass through the waters, I shall be
    with you;
or through rivers, they will not swallow you up.
Should you walk through fire, you will not
    suffer,
and the flame will not burn you.
For I am Yahweh, your God, the Holy One of
    Israel, your Saviour . . .
Since I regard you as precious, and I love you
. . .
Do not be afraid, for I am with you.

(Isaiah 43:1-3, 4, 5)

Jesus heals our hearts through the gift of the Spirit, and then he calls us in turn to work towards the creation of communities of love; a church of compassion, more committed to living in solidarity with others, particularly with the poor; and a society where people struggle to bring peace and justice.

Kneeling before his disciples, Jesus is testifying not only to his love for each one, but also to his desire to eliminate the fears and barriers of domination that exist between those who act like masters and those who work like slaves; between all those who refuse to look further than their own group and culture. Jesus yearns to bring together in unity all the scattered children of God; to bring them into the same unity he lives with the Father. The cry and thirst of his heart is revealed in his final prayer to the Father:

> May they all be one, just as, Father, you are in me and I am in you,
> may they also be in us,
> so that the world may believe it was you who sent me.
> I have given them the glory you gave to me,
> that they may be one as we are one.
> With me in them and you in me,
> may they be so perfected in unity that the world will recognize
> that it was you who sent me
> and that you have loved them as you have loved me.   (John 17:20-23)

Jesus suffers when he sees people crush and dominate others, especially the weak, the poor and people with handicaps. He cannot accept prejudice against the poor, or against those who are "different," those who are "strangers," belonging to another race, religion or culture. He cannot accept prejudice against the sick; or of men against women (and the reverse). Jesus loves each person no matter what his or her culture, race, limits or weakness may be. For him, each person is important; each one is "holy ground"; each one is part of a common humanity.

Jesus came to eliminate war and oppression. He wants each person to be able to live free from fear and from the powers of evil. He wants us to be free to love and to be open and welcoming to others, especially those who are different. Each person has his or her place in the body of humanity. This is what Jesus demonstrates as he washes his disciples' feet.

In Paul's letter to the Ephesians he explains Jesus' mission of peace by speaking of the unity which Jesus creates between the Jews and the Gentiles:

> For he is the peace between us,
> and has made the two into one
> and broken down the barriers which used to keep them apart,
> by destroying in his own person the hostility,
> that is, the Law of commandments with its decrees.
> His purpose in this was, by restoring peace,
> to create a single New Person out of the two of them,

and through the cross, to reconcile them both to
God in one Body;
in his own person he killed the hostility.
He came to bring the good news of peace to you
who were far off
and peace to those who were near.
Through him, then, we both in the one Spirit
have free access to the Father.

(Ephesians 2:14 ff.)

In his letter to the Corinthian community Paul speaks of Jesus' vision for humanity, how each person is a part of the body which is the Church. In this body, each part is unique, each is different. There is no more competition or jealousy, no more fear or rejection of difference. There are no more barriers. Each one is there to help others find their place and everyone should give preference to others (cf. Philippians 2:3). Just as the eye needs the ear and the foot, each part of the body needs the other parts. Paul adds that: "It is precisely the parts that seem to be the weakest which are the indispensable ones. It is the parts that we consider least dignified that we surround with the greatest dignity; and our less presentable parts are given greater presentability" (1 Corinthians 12:22-24). Is Paul not talking here about the place people with handicaps should have in the Church?

The Poor: Source of Unity

Jesus knows the pain of those who are outcast. Feeling rejected, they lose all confidence in themselves. They are closed up in a negative image of themselves and bound by a sense of guilt. The poor cry out for love and communion. That is why they are so close to God. They cry out for God, since God is love and communion. They cry out for unity.

Jesus, humble and poor, stripped of his clothes and washing his friends' feet, shows that the poor and the weak can become a source of unity. Good leaders, if they are attentive to each person, can be instruments of unity by creating good and just laws and regulations. They call forth other people's understanding and goodwill. The poor, the weak, and the suffering create unity by awakening people's hearts. Weakness and littleness can attract hearts, like a baby in a family can be a source of unity for a family. When there are natural catastrophes, people of different classes, backgrounds and religions often join together to help those in distress and solidarity is born. Hearts are sensitive to suffering and frequently respond with generosity.

We in L'Arche have often witnessed how people from different backgrounds come together in order to help those in need. In Bethany, in the West Bank, where we used to have a L'Arche community, Christians from Western countries and Palestinian Muslims lived and worked together for the good of our people with handicaps. By his humble presence in the poor, Jesus makes us penetrate into the mystery of the poor as a source of unity. This coincides with Paul's vision of the Church as a body where the weak and suffering are necessary and should be held in honour (cf. 1 Corinthians 12).

A Gradual Transformation of the Heart

In L'Arche we constantly need to renew our awareness of the gift we have been given: the poor and the weak must be at the heart of our communities, for they have been entrusted to us by God. They are called by God to be at the centre of the new society, the new creation, which is not really a society but a body. If we are to become part of this body, if we are to stop seeking the best place and accept our place, our gift and our mission, as well as those of others, we need a change of heart and a new inner attitude. This change is like a new birth, a transformation where we let go of our usual guidelines and security. Jesus offers us this transformation. Our hearts of stone, full of fear and blockages, can be transformed into hearts of flesh, open, compassionate and vulnerable, through the gentle power of the Holy Spirit as promised by the prophets and Jesus.

I shall pour clean water over you and you will be cleansed;
I shall cleanse you of all your filth and of your

foul idols.

I shall give you a new heart and put a new spirit
in you;

I shall remove the heart of stone from your
bodies

and give you a heart of flesh instead.

I shall put my spirit in you, and make you keep
my laws,

and respect and practise my judgements.

You will live in the country which I gave your
ancestors.

You will be my people and I shall be your God.

(Ezekiel 36:25-28)

This transformation, given through a sense of
God's loving presence in our lives, is never instan-
taneous; it takes time. It is like a tiny seed planted in
the earth of our being. In the beginning, we may
have a strong experience, a meeting with God, a call
to follow Jesus and to give our lives to him. This
experience is given to those who are open and
humble enough to receive it. God brings down the
powerful from their thrones and raises up the
humble. This is what the man in Mark's Gospel
experienced when "Jesus looked at him and loved
him" (Mark 10:21). Jesus called the man to follow
him, to let go of what he possessed and give himself
completely to Jesus. But this man couldn't let go of
his security; he was frightened and turned away
from Jesus. Many people who have possessions and

power cannot accept this transformation; they are too frightened or self-satisfied. They risk protecting themselves behind cultural and material comforts. They hide behind firm beliefs, apparently sure of their way of seeing things, incapable of questioning themselves and their prejudices. Jesus, kneeling before his disciples, reminds us that, in order to enter his kingdom of love, we need to be humble and to have the trusting heart of a child. We need to take the step from holding onto our own personal security, to finding security in the Holy Spirit.

The seed of the Spirit, planted in the soil of our being, must be received and nourished if it is to grow. It has to be protected from the seductions and worries of the world. It must be allowed always to penetrate more deeply into our hearts which are both yearning for Jesus and afraid of union with him. We realize that as we follow Jesus we will lose a certain freedom and control over our own lives. We will know loss and grief and we will have to let go of some of our own ideas. It is a little like people who get married: they lose their independence, but gain a new freedom.

Loss and grief will be with us our whole life through, because growth in Jesus' love is a long process that involves struggle. This struggle is not so much against disobeying moral laws and commandments, but the struggle to trust in Jesus' call, in his promises of love and his invitation to give our lives totally to him. It is the struggle to let the Holy Spirit take over our lives, guide and inspire us in all we do. It is a struggle to remain constantly open and faithful to the Holy Spirit on this new path of love.

And no matter how beautiful a community may be, community life still remains difficult, due to all our inner resistance and our need to feel important. There is such a fear in us of not existing if we are not held in esteem and this fear will remain with us all our lives. Transformation takes time and continues through times of joy and times of purification, until our last breath.

5

PETER AND JUDAS: A REVELATION OF THE HEART

At the Last Supper, there are two protagonists, two people in contradiction with Jesus: Peter and Judas.

Peter's Confusion

We can understand Peter's reaction: "No, you will not wash my feet, never!" He cannot accept the fact that Jesus would kneel down before him and serve him. Peter's inner world is shattered. He was used to a vision of politics and religion where the leader is on top, a rock that he could lean on and that gave security. Peter followed Jesus because the latter appeared to be strong: he performed miracles, nourished the crowd, healed the sick, raised Lazarus from the dead. Jesus had been transformed in front of Peter on Mount Tabor. He spoke with authority and responded with force to the scribes and the Pharisees. Peter believed that Jesus was the Messiah. It wasn't difficult to give up his former life to follow such a powerful, charismatic leader. Peter admired Jesus' strength. Here was a man, he thought, who would expel the Romans from Israel, unify the people, and give them back their freedom and dignity. And now he sees this same Jesus kneeling humbly in front of him! Peter never imagined a Messiah like that! Because of his own limits and weaknesses, Peter needed a strong leader, a rock, someone he could admire.

Peter's confusion only increases when, early the next morning, Jesus is arrested and brought before the Sanhedrin to be judged. Jesus no longer defends himself; he remains silent. His hands are tied together. Peter just cannot come to terms with the fact that Jesus would let himself be defeated like that; he cannot admit that the scribes and Pharisees, these mediocre religious leaders, would win, and, with them, the Romans. Peter collapses. When the servant comes to him and says: "You were also one of his disciples," Peter protests and swears: "No! I do not know that man!"

Peter is not a man who is easily frightened. He is a broken man. He had thought Jesus would be the strong Messiah, and now he sees that he is weak. Peter had an ideal of strength, generosity, and truth;

an ideal where the good win and the bad lose. He feels now that he has been deceived. It is similar to a man marrying and finding a few years later that the woman he married is not what he thought she was. Or to a woman joining a community that she idealizes, and then discovering all the conflicts and underlying hypocrisy in the community and in individual members. Peter revolts. Jesus has betrayed him; his disappointment is immense. How could the Messiah be so weak? The Messiah is supposed to be there to solve all problems, to answer all needs, especially if we are open and obedient to God. Who is this Messiah who, after kneeling down like a servant or a slave, allows himself to be attacked and insulted? It's absurd! It's a scandal! Peter finds it too much to bear, just as he couldn't bear Jesus' words when he said:

> Anyone who does eat my flesh and drink my blood has eternal life,
> and I shall raise that person up on the last day.
> For my flesh is real food and my blood real drink.
> Whoever eats my flesh and drinks my blood
> lives in me and I live in that person.
>
> (John 6:54-56)

Jesus had spoken these words just when the crowd was beginning to believe in him, after the feeding of the five thousand. Now the crowd is shocked and scandalized by these words, the idea of eating his body and drinking his blood! Impossible! Intolerable! "After hearing it, many of his followers said, 'This is intolerable language. How could anyone accept it?' After this, many of his disciples went away and accompanied him no more" (John 6:60-66).

We can well understand the disciples' confusion and anger. Why did Jesus talk like that just when everyone was starting to believe in him and to follow him? What an intolerable mistake!

In reaction to the crowd's unbelief, perhaps Jesus had tears in his eyes when he said to the apostles: "Are you going to leave me too?" He knew their confusion and desperation. When he shares with them what is most intimate, the deepest secret of his heart, his desire to be their friend, the disciples are shaken. They want a strong Messiah, not a vulnerable one. They want a Messiah who will liberate their people, not one who offers love and a heart-to-heart relationship of communion. Peter cannot understand, but he is loyal, faithful and, above all, he trusts in Jesus: "Lord, to whom shall we go? Yours are the words of eternal life" (John 6:68).

Jesus' disciples today, just as in the past, have trouble understanding God who becomes poor and humble, hidden in the weak and the poor, and in people with handicaps like Loïc. How can we understand a God who is so great that he can become little and vulnerable in order to touch people's hearts and to live a relationship of love with each one? God's all-powerfulness is hidden in order to show that it is a power of love and in order to awaken the powers of love in each one of us, if we are open and humble and trusting. Isn't there something intolerable and scandalous about a God who becomes weak?

Later that evening Jesus announces that he will soon be leaving them:

> But now I am going to the one who sent me. . . .
> Yet you are sad at heart because I have told you this.
> Still, I am telling you the truth:
> it is for your own good that I am going,
> because unless I go, the Paraclete will not come to you;
> but if I go, I will send him to you.
>
> (John 16:5-7)

If the teacher stays, the disciples remain disciples and followers; if he leaves, they in turn will become teachers, gentle and humble like Jesus, full of passionate love for each human being. This can only be accomplished by the Holy Spirit who will transform them and give them a whole new way of seeing and doing things.

If Jesus washes Peter's feet, then Peter too will be called to become little and vulnerable, like a servant. He will be called to wash others' feet and to build a new society, a community of love where the weak are at the centre. Peter will become a servant of servants. But in order to do that, he must give up certain ideas and even holy customs and traditions that gave him security. He will have to let God guide him in all things and to new things. He will have to pass through a dark night of not understanding. He must live "the cloud of unknowing." Peter finds it difficult to accept this transformation. Yet he allows Jesus to wash his feet, even if he cannot understand. By becoming flesh, the Word makes all things new: he brings a new vision of humanity, a new way of being. God is no longer revealed just in the heavens, but God is more particularly present in the earth, hidden in the earth of pain and of poverty, and hidden in the earth of our own being. Mary, Jesus' mother, lived this radical change at the moment of the Incarnation, when the Word became flesh. For her, God was not just in the Temple of Jerusalem and in the prophets' words, but she found a new presence of God in the body of her child, and in her own body. This is a radically new path.

Judas's Betrayal

Peter may not understand Jesus, but he loves him and finally gives in to him. After denying Jesus, Peter realizes what he has done and cries bitterly. During the washing of the feet Judas does not intervene, but his presence creates a tension, a feeling of uneasiness. Throughout the text one senses Judas like a heavy cloud over them all: "They were at supper, and the devil had already put into the mind of Judas Iscariot, son of Simon, to betray him . . ." (John 13:2).

Still later, Jesus says,

No one who has had a bath needs washing;
such a person is clean all over.
You too are clean, though not all of you are.
(John 13:10-11)

And then Jesus adds,

I am not speaking about all of you:
I know the ones I have chosen;
but what scripture says must be fulfilled:
'He who shares my table, takes advantage of me.'
I tell you this now, before it happens,
so that when it does happen, you may believe that I am he.   (John 13:18-19)

And later still, John tells us, "Having said this, Jesus was deeply disturbed and declared, 'In all truth I tell you, one of you is going to betray me.' After Judas had taken the bread from Jesus, Satan entered him" (John 13:21-27).

John shows us three different moments when Judas appears in contradiction with Jesus. The first, which we have already quoted, is when Jesus speaks of his body to be eaten and his blood to be drunk. Peter responds:

"Lord, to whom shall we go?
You have the message of eternal life . . ."
Jesus replied: "Did I not choose the twelve of you?
Yet one of you is a devil."
He meant Judas son of Simon Iscariot, since this was the man,
one of the twelve, who was to betray him.

(John 6:67-71)

The second episode is when Martha's sister Mary poured precious ointment on Jesus' feet in Bethany, which made Judas angry: "'Why was this ointment not sold for three hundred denarii and the money given to the poor?' He said this, not because he cared about the poor, but because he was a thief" (John 12:4-6).

What do these two events and the washing of the feet have in common? Why do they provoke such a negative reaction in Judas? In each of these situations Jesus appears weak and vulnerable, in search of communion. He no longer looks like the strong, powerful Messiah who is going to liberate the Jewish people. Judas cannot accept this weak, gentle and vulnerable Jesus who loves and calls others to a communion of love. Judas wants action. He wants struggle and power. He wants to be with a powerful Jesus and to have his share of that power.

Perhaps Peter has the same temptation, but more fundamentally he trusts Jesus. He is not completely blocked by Jesus' call to love and communion, even if he does not fully understand. Judas' reaction shows, however, that there might be serious psychological and spiritual blockages in him with regard to communion and love. Perhaps he is jealous of any intimate relationship Jesus has that does not include him. This jealousy and revolt against a gentle, loving Jesus pave the way for the devil to enter his heart. Satan then can take over and inspire Judas to betray Jesus and hand him over.

6

Conclusion

This image of Jesus kneeling at the feet of humanity has been with me for some time now. Jesus stooping down to cleanse and heal the wounds, and to wash the feet, not saying anything, but with tears rolling down his cheeks. What a difference from the image of God as a judge who rules, condemns and punishes; a God who sees human beings as guilty. People have had that image of God for centuries. But Jesus tells us: "Come to me, all you who labour and are overburdened, and I will give you rest" (Matthew 11:28).

Today people are worn out. There is so much to learn, so much to do. Competition is everywhere, where a few win and many others lose. Life is a constant struggle to survive. Many people have to wear masks so that no one sees their discouragement, their heart's pain, their desperation because they lack a sense of their own dignity and because, sometimes, they lack work.

Other people are tired by the long hours of travel to and from work, by their over-full agendas, things to do, success to achieve and by all the unresolved social problems and world problems. When people are too tired and fragmented, they no longer have the energy or the desire to celebrate and give thanks. They have no time to reach out to others, especially to the poor and the marginalized and to open their hearts to them.

In L'Arche I discovered what communion of the heart means. Before, I used to flee relationships. I was quite austere, and organized my life around studies and prayer. I was frightened of becoming too vulnerable. I protected myself. I always had to do things, to know what to do, to control and to teach. I had learned how to help others like a superior who knew what to do in order to make others happy and to put them on the right path. My heart was open to God but closed to other people as they were, and in their most fundamental needs. It took time for me to learn that you cannot really open your heart to God without opening it to others. John, the beloved disciple of Jesus, says:

Beloved, let us love one another since love is from God,
and everyone who loves is a child of God and

knows God.
Whoever fails to love does not know God
because God is love.
Anyone who says "I love God" and hates his or
her brother or sister is a liar,
since whoever does not love the person whom
he or she can see
cannot love God whom he or she has not seen.
Indeed this is the commandment we have
received from him (Jesus)
that whoever loves God, must also love his or
her brother or sister.

(I John 4:7-8, 20)

Jesus brought me close to people suffering from
mental handicaps. They called me to take another
path, the path of tenderness, compassion and communion. They taught me how to celebrate. As I
shared my life with them, I discovered the importance of listening and of communicating through
non-verbal as well as verbal language. I could not
treat them according to my usual norms in working
with students who were there to be taught. Raphael
and Philippe and each of the others wanted something else from me: they wanted friendship, which
implies understanding. I had to try to listen to their
heartbeat, understand their greatest needs, and discover what would help them find meaning in life,
and hope and trust in themselves. They led me to
communion of the heart. However, in order to live

this new love and communion faithfully, I needed a new gift of the Holy Spirit.

In L'Arche, I was given the gift of the beauty, the gentleness, the purity of heart and the trust of Raphael, Philippe and many others, as well as their pain. The child hidden in their hearts awakened the child within me. There were, of course, moments when I continued to act like the navy officer I had been and I gave orders. Sometimes that was good and even necessary, but sometimes it was just my need to control and find security. There was, and still is, a struggle in me, between the need to be right, to control and to have all the answers, and the call to welcome others, simply to be with them, to accept them just as they are and to have confidence in them and in God. There is still a struggle in me between the need to go up in order to command, and the call to go down, to listen to love, and to be vulnerable with others.

Jesus washing the disciples' feet shows us how God loves and how his disciples, then as now, are called to love and to love "to the very end."

The washing of the feet is finally a mystery, like so many of Jesus' acts. We enter into this mystery gradually, through events in which we suffer loss and are stripped more and more of all we possess. When Jesus tells Peter that he will understand "later," Jesus is telling all of his disciples that it is only after a dark night of not knowing, and only

82

through a new gift of the Holy Spirit, that we can penetrate this mystery and live it.

Jesus invites his friends to lay down the garments which give them a special status, to remove the masks that hide their real selves and to present themselves to others humbly, vulnerably, with all their poverty. To become humble and small requires a loving heart, purified of its fears and human security, ready to love to the end, in order to give life to others.

How does Jesus want us to imitate him? Jesus is asking us to follow him on a path of littleness, forgiveness, trust, communion and vulnerability – without giving up at other moments our role of responsibility where we exercise authority with force and justice, kindness and firmness. Jesus invites us to live the folly of the Gospel, not to judge others, but to be compassionate, to forgive and to love to the end, even to loving our enemies. This is impossible unless we remove our garments and become poor and naked before God, in order to be more fully "clothed in Christ."

Some people, inspired by the Holy Spirit, live more fully the blessedness of the washing of feet and eating with the poor, the lame, the crippled and the blind. Others who carry important responsibilities in society are touched by Jesus' sermon on the mountain and the example of his life; they yearn to follow him more closely. Every Maundy Thursday,

King Louis IX of France – St. Louis – used to wash the feet of the sick. He liked to receive beggars into his house and would serve them at table. One day while he was walking with an escort, they heard the sound of a leper's bell. His escort ran away, frightened of the contact with the leper. Louis however went to meet the leper and kissed his hand. Whenever Mahatma Gandhi visited a city, he would always stay with the "untouchables" whose name he changed to *harijans*, "children of God." In his own community life in the ashram, even when he had an important role in politics, he made a point of washing the toilets – and he did this until the end of his life. In this way he was a privileged witness to Jesus, humble and poor, Jesus the servant whom he admired so much.

It is up to each of us to discover how he or she is called to be more fully "clothed in Christ," in order for us to serve our brothers and sisters with love, kindness and humility. It is up to each one to come closer to those who are "below," to help them stand up, to listen to them, to ask their advice, to meet them just as they are, with all their differences, to be one with them.

Jesus insists that the disciples wash each other's feet. He tells Peter that it is not optional but absolutely necessary to have his feet washed by Jesus, otherwise "you will have no part in me." Jesus affirms that, by doing this, he is giving us all an example to be followed, and that it is a beatitude, a blessing. All this is certainly because Jesus wants us to have an inner attitude of humility and service at all times. But he is also affirming the importance of actually washing each other's feet. This act of humility expresses in a very concrete way our love and respect for others.

Isn't this the logic of the sacraments? Each one signifies physically a gift of life and of love. The water of baptism cleanses us and gives us new life; the consecrated bread, broken, given and eaten, and the consecrated wine, offered and consumed, are all signs through which Jesus gives himself to us, so that we may live continually in communion with him, in a heart-to-heart relationship. The sacraments are signs of the gift and at the same time are real instruments of the gift, as long as we receive them with faith, trust and love; Jesus cannot give himself to us unless we welcome him into our hearts.

During the Maundy Thursday liturgy in the Roman Catholic Church, the priest washes the feet of twelve people in the congregation, as a sign of obedience to Jesus. Isn't Jesus asking all the members of all Christian communities, of all Christian families, to wash each other's feet in a well-prepared ceremony, in a spirit of prayer, service and communion?

To wash the feet of a brother or sister in Christ, to allow someone to wash our feet, is a sign that together we want to follow Jesus, to take the downward path, to find Jesus' presence in the poor and the weak. Is it not a sign that we too want to live a heart-to-heart relationship with others, to meet them as a person and a friend, and to live in communion with them? Is it not a sign also that we yearn to be men and women of forgiveness, to be healed and cleansed and to heal and cleanse others and thus to live more fully in communion with Jesus?

AGMV
MARQUIS
Québec, Canada
1998